3rd Edition

FULL VOICE®
WORKBOOK SERIES

LEVEL ONE

Researched and Developed
by Nikki Loney and Mim Adams

www.thefullvoice.com

© 2018 FULL VOICE MUSIC
All Rights Reserved
ISBN: 978-1-897539-13-2
FVM-L1

Welcome to the 3rd Edition FULL VOICE Workbook Series

These workbooks have been researched and developed for singers working with a vocal teacher in private or classroom lessons. Every FULL VOICE lesson has fun and educational activities that encourage vocal students to sing, listen, read and write music. These workbooks complement any lesson regardless of the teaching style or repertoire preferred by student or teacher.

Introductory Level - For students ages 5-7 who are new to music lessons.

Level One - For students who have completed the Introductory Level, or the starting level for students ages 7 and up who have introductory music lesson experience (private, classroom or choral). Also suitable for older students who are new to music lessons.

Level Two - For students who have completed Level One, or students who are confident counting eighth notes and sight singing in C Major.

Level Three - For students who have completed Level Two, or students who are confident counting dotted quarter notes, singing and identifying intervals and sight singing in C, F, and G Major.

The FULL VOICE Teacher Guide

A soft cover book with 102 pages of teaching inspiration and strategies for the private voice teacher. It includes:

- simple and effective teaching strategies that you can use immediately.
- helpful strategies for getting started with new students and first lessons.
- multi-sensory warm-up activities for singers of all abilities.
- MORE singing games for beginner singers to help develop independent singing skills from the very first lesson.
- NEW! FULL VOICE Small group lesson curriculum and planning.
- NEW! Age appropriate repertoire recommendations for young singers.

Acknowledgements
Thank you to all the students, teachers, and parents who have participated in the FULL VOICE test groups over the past ten years. We are truly grateful to all the print music specialists and music retailers that have supported the FULL VOICE Workbook Series since the first edition printing in 2004.

FVM-IL	ISBN	978-1-897539-12-5	FULL VOICE Workbook - Introductory Level
FVM-L1	ISBN	978-1-897539-13-2	FULL VOICE Workbook - Level One
FVM-L2	ISBN	978-1-897539-14-9	FULL VOICE Workbook - Level Two
FVM-L3	ISBN	978-1-897539-15-6	FULL VOICE Workbook - Level Three

TABLE OF CONTENTS

TONIC SOL-FA REVIEW

Date: _____

DO

Tonic sol-fa is a singing method that uses words and hand signs for every note in a scale. Tonic sol-fa is very easy to learn and the first step towards learning to sight sing. Tonic sol-fa can be a lot of fun!

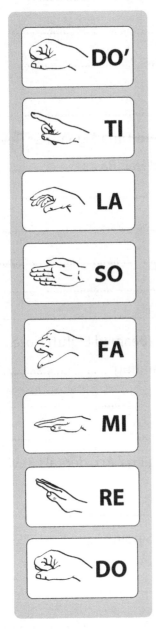

DO'
TI
LA
SO
FA
MI
RE
DO

1. Sing and sign the tonic sol-fa scale.

a) Sing and sign **repeating** notes.

 DO   **DO**   **DO**

Repeating notes remain on the same pitch.

b) Sing and sign **ascending**.

 DO   **RE**   **MI**

Ascending means that the pitch moves **higher**.

c) Sing and sign **descending**.

 MI   **RE**   **DO**

Descending means that the pitch moves **lower**.

2. Listen carefully as your teacher plays or hums melodies that repeat, ascend or descend.

☐ I can identify repeating, ascending and descending notes.

1. Write the correct tonic sol-fa syllable below each hand sign.

a)

DO _____ _____ _____ _____

b)

_____ _____ _____ _____ _____

2. Fill in the missing tonic sol-fa syllables.

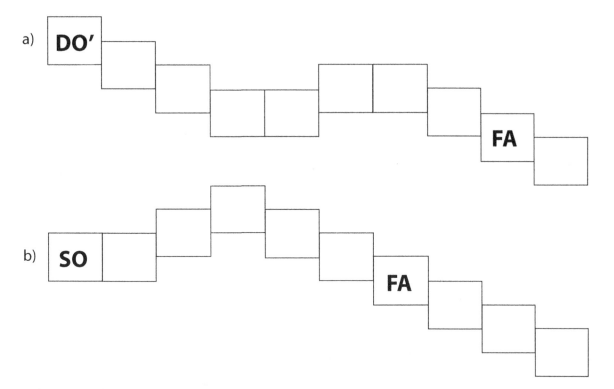

a) **DO'** ... **FA**

b) **SO** ... **FA**

LESSON REVIEW: TONIC SOL-FA SCALE

1. ☐ Practice singing and signing the tonic sol-fa scale ascending.

2. ☐ Practice singing and signing the tonic sol-fa scale descending.

3. ☐ Sing the tonic sol-fa scale ascending and descending from memory. *(5 marks)*

_____
5

Lesson Two

TONIC SOL-FA

Date: _____

DO'	
TI	
LA	
SO	
FA	
MI	
RE	
DO	

1. 🗣 Review the tonic sol-fa scale with your teacher.

2. ✓ Check when completed.

☐ I can sing and sign the scale **ascending**.

☐ I can sing and sign the scale **descending**.

☐ I can sing the scale **ascending and descending in one breath.**

3. 🗣 Sing the following tonic sol-fa patterns *without* signing.

a) **DO DO DO RE MI**

b) **DO RE MI FA SO**

c) **DO RE DO RE MI**

4. ✏ Write your own tonic sol-fa melody.

5. 🗣 Sing your melody.

☐ ☐ ☐ ☐ ☐

LEARNING NOTES REVIEW

Music is written using symbols called **notes**. Each note is played or sung using **counts** or **beats**. Like the ticking of a clock, the beats or counting of music is always **steady**.

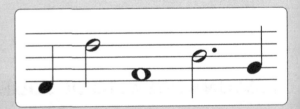

1. ✓ Check when completed.

☐ I can clap a steady beat with my teacher.

☐ I can clap a steady beat by myself.

quarter note

𝅘𝅥

1

A quarter note is held for **one beat** or count.

1. Clap and count **quarter notes**.
2. Sing **quarter notes** using **DO**, **RE,** or **MI**.
3. Practice drawing **quarter notes**.

half note

𝅗𝅥

1 2

A half note is held for **two beats** or counts.

4. Clap and count **half notes**.
5. Sing **half notes** using **DO**, **RE,** or **MI**.
6. Practice drawing **half notes**.

whole note

𝅝

1 2 3 4

A whole note is held for **four beats** or counts.

7. Clap and count **whole notes**.
8. Sing **whole notes** using **DO**, **RE,** or **MI**.
9. Practice drawing **whole notes**.

dotted half note

𝅗𝅥.

1 2 3

A dotted half note is held for **three beats** or counts.

10. Clap and count **dotted half notes**.
11. Practice drawing **dotted half notes**.

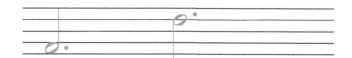

Lesson Three

TONIC SOL-FA

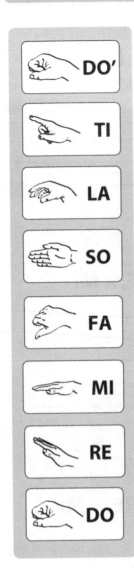

DO'
TI
LA
SO
FA
MI
RE
DO

1. Sing and sign the tonic sol-fa scale ascending and descending.

2. Sing and sign the tonic sol-fa scale ascending and descending without looking at your book.

3. Sing the following tonic sol-fa patterns *without* signing.

a) **DO   DO   RE   DO   RE**

b) **DO   RE   MI   RE   DO**

c) **DO   RE   RE   MI   MI**

4. Sign a tonic sol-fa melody for your teacher to sing.

CLAPPING AND COUNTING

1. Write the counts under each note.
2. Clap and count the notes slowly.

a)

1   1   2

b)

c)

d)

Music is written on a **staff**.
This staff has five lines
and four spaces.

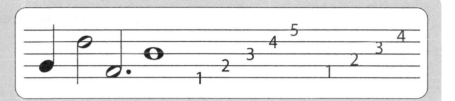

1. Draw a **whole note** on every line.

2. Draw a **whole note** in each space.

There is a symbol that is found at the beginning of the staff. This is called a **clef**. Music for *most* singers is written using the **treble clef**.

This clef is also called the **G clef**. It is a fancy capital "**G**". When drawn onto the staff, it curls around the second line.

3. **Trace** the steps to learn to draw the **treble clef**.

LESSON REVIEW: MUSIC STAFF AND TREBLE CLEF

1. ✓ Look at the music below.

   a) Circle all the notes that are written on **lines**. *(5 marks)*

   b) How many **half notes** are there? _____ *(1 mark)*

2. Practice drawing **treble clefs** on the staff. *(4 marks)*

10

TONIC SOL-FA

Date: _____

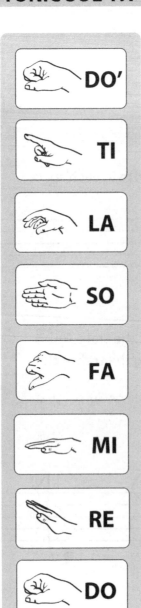

DO'

TI

LA

SO

FA

MI

RE

DO

1. Sing the entire scale **ascending** and **descending**.

2. Sing and sign the following.

a)

b)

3. Sing the following:

a) **DO DO DO RE MI**

b) **DO RE MI FA SO**

4. ✓ Look carefully at the sol-fa melody examples below.

5. Listen carefully as your teacher hums one of the melodies. Can you identify the correct melody?

a) **DO DO RE RE**   b) **DO RE MI MI**

c) **MI RE RE DO**   d) **DO RE MI RE**

TREBLE CLEF REVIEW

1. Draw five treble clefs on the staff. Circle the best one.

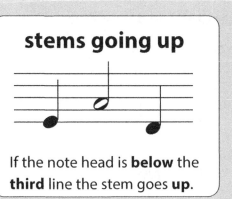

stems going up

If the note head is **below** the **third** line the stem goes **up**.

1. Draw stems going **up**.

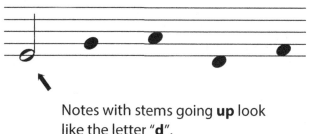

Notes with stems going **up** look like the letter "**d**".

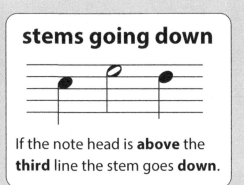

stems going down

If the note head is **above** the **third** line the stem goes **down**.

2. Draw stems going **down**.

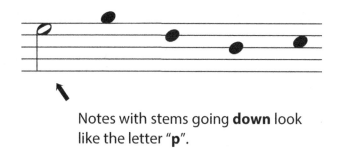

Notes with stems going **down** look like the letter "**p**".

The stems on the notes **on line 3** can go **up or down**. Notice how the stems go through the staff.

3. Add stems in the direction indicated.

UP   DOWN   DOWN   UP   DOWN

LESSON REVIEW: WRITING STEMS

1. Add the correct stem to each note. *(7 marks)*

7

Lesson Five

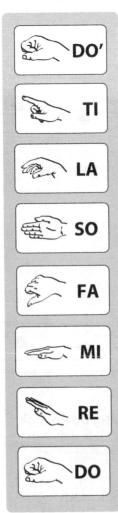

DO'

TI

LA

SO

FA

MI

RE

DO

1.  Sing the entire scale **ascending** and **descending**.

2. Sing the sol-fa using the correct rhythm.

a)

DO RE DO   RE MI

b)

DO   RE MI MI   FA

MUSICAL ALPHABET REVIEW

In music we use only the first seven letters of the alphabet. These letters repeat over and over.

A B C D E F G

1. Fill in the missing letters. Remember that they repeat over and over.

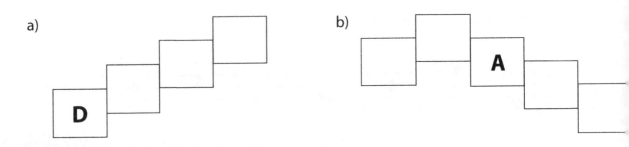

a)

D

b)

A

The note names on the music staff move up in steps. Notice that they move from **line to space to line**. These seven letters repeat over and over.

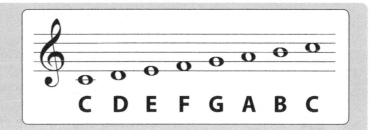

1.  Copy the **treble clef** and the **musical alphabet** from above.

---

middle C

It sits **below** the staff

2. Practice drawing **middle C** on the staff.

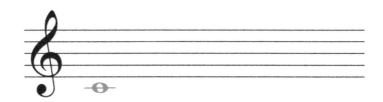

D

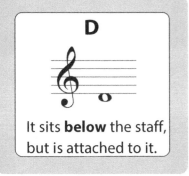

It sits **below** the staff, but is attached to it.

3. Practice drawing **D** on the staff.

LESSON REVIEW: MIDDLE C AND D

1. Practice writing **middle C** and **D** using **quarter notes** and **half notes**.

10

Review One

TONIC SOL-FA

Date: _____

DO'
TI
LA
SO
FA
MI
RE
DO

1. ✓ Check when completed. *(1 mark each)*

☐ I can sing and sign the entire scale ascending.

☐ I can sing and sign the entire scale descending.

☐ I can sing and sign the entire scale ascending and descending.

☐ I can sing the entire scale ascending and descending in one breath.

2. 🖊 Fill in the missing tonic sol-fa syllables. *(7 marks)*

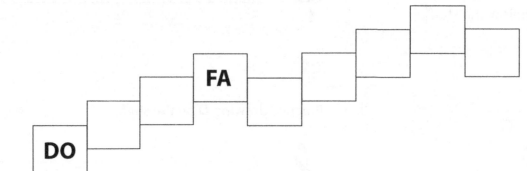

3. 🗣 Sing the tonic sol-fa with the correct rhythm. *(3 marks each)*

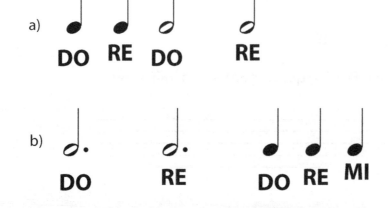

a) DO RE DO RE

b) DO RE DO RE MI

14

4. Draw lines connecting the notes, names and number of beats. *(7 marks)*

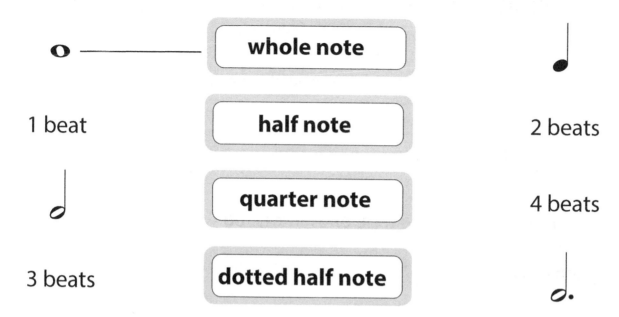

5. Add a stem to each note. *(5 marks)*

6. Write the letters that make up the musical alphabet. *(1 mark)*

7. a) Draw a treble clef on the staff. *(1 mark)*

b) Write the note middle C below the staff. *(1 mark)*

c) Write the note D below the staff. *(1 mark)*

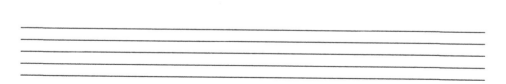

16   30

Lesson Six

VOWEL SOUNDS

Date: _____

EE AH OH OO

When singing exercises, singers use **vowel sounds**. Pay close attention to the shape of your mouth and the sound of your vowels.

1. Sing the following exercises using round, open **vowel sounds**.

a)

EE as in ME. **AH** as in FATHER. **OH** as in NOTE. **OO** as in BOOT.

LINE NOTES REVIEW

The letter names of the notes on the staff **lines** make a sentence that is easy to remember.

Every **G**ood **B**oy **D**eserves **F**un

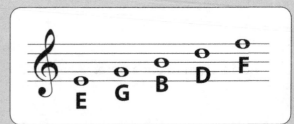

1. Draw a **treble clef** at the beginning of the staff.
2. Identify the **line** notes.

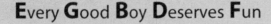

3. Draw a **treble clef** at the beginning of the staff.
4. Write the notes on the staff. Use **half notes**.

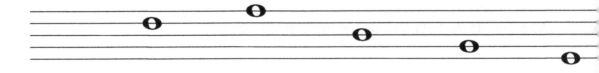

B	C	E	G	D	F

The letter names of the notes in the staff **spaces** spell a word that is easy to remember.

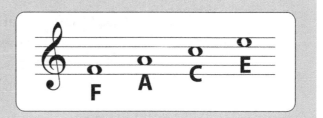

F A C E

1. Draw a **treble clef** at the beginning of the staff.
2. Identify the **space** notes.

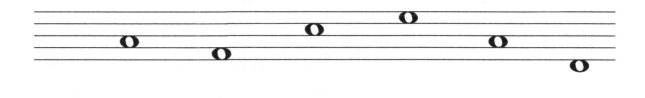

3. Draw a **treble clef** at the beginning of the staff.
4. Write the notes on the staff. Use **half notes**.

B   G   F   C   A   E

LESSON REVIEW: NOTE NAMES

1. Name the **line** notes. *(6 marks)*

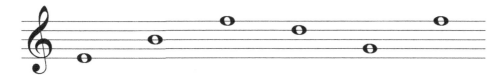

2. Name the **space** notes. *(6 marks)*

$\overline{12}$

Lesson Seven

SINGING LEGATO

Date: _____

legato

Sing legato! Legato means smooth and connected.
Singers need to breathe deeply to sing legato. Your teacher
will demonstrate.

1. Sing the following exercise using relaxed, open vowel sounds.

a)

The curved line connecting the notes is called a **slur**.
It tells us to sing **legato** - smooth and connected.

NOTE NAMING CHALLENGE

1. Draw a **treble clef** at the beginning of each staff.

2. Have your teacher time you. How fast can you name your notes?

☐ 40-60 seconds (Not bad)   ☐ 25-40 seconds (Good)

☐ 15-25 seconds (Great)   ☐ 10-15 seconds (Amazing!)

SONG INTRODUCTIONS

 Your performance begins *before* you sing your song. You have to welcome your audience, tell them who you are and share some information about the song you are about to perform. Here is an example of a very basic introduction.

1. 💬 Greet the audience. *"Good evening, ladies and gentlemen…"*

2. 💬 Introduce yourself. *"My name is _____."*

3. 💬 Tell the audience about your song. *"Tonight I will be performing _____."*

4. ✓ Practice your basic introduction for you teacher. Remember the following:

   ☐ Stand confidently with proper posture. ☐ Speak slowly and enunciate clearly.

   ☐ Project your voice into the audience. ☐ Smile.

5. ✓ Use an introduction every time you perform.

PERFORMANCE ASSESSMENT # 1

Choose one memorized song and perform it for your teacher.

Performance will be marked accordingly:
     A Great job – keep up the good work.
     B Good job – still room to improve.
     C Needs work – improvement needed here.

Song: _____

1. Did the singer appear comfortable and confident?	**A**	**B**	**C**
2. Did the singer sing/speak clearly throughout the song?	**A**	**B**	**C**
3. Were the vowel sounds open and round?	**A**	**B**	**C**
4. Did the singer perform all notes and rhythms accurately?	**A**	**B**	**C**
5. Did the performer use an introduction?	**A**	**B**	**C**
6. _____	**A**	**B**	**C**

Teacher comments:

Lesson Eight

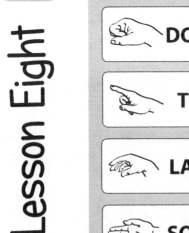

 DO'

 **TI**

 **LA**

 **SO**

 **FA**

 **MI**

 **RE**

 **DO**

TONIC SOL-FA
Date: _____

1.  Sing the scale using tonic sol-fa syllables.
2.  Sing the scale using the vowel **AH**.
3. Sing the following.

a   **DO   RE   MI   RE   DO**

b) **DO   RE   MI   FA   SO**

c) **DO   RE   MI   FA   DO**

d) **DO   RE   RE   MI   DO**

4. Write your own tonic sol-fa melody.
5.  Have your teacher sing your melody.

☐ ☐ ☐ ☐ ☐

MELODIC SING-BACK

1. Listen carefully while your teacher plays the following two bar melodies **twice**.
2. Sing the melody back using "loo".

a)  ☐

b)  ☐

BAR LINES, MEASURES AND TIME SIGNATURES REVIEW

Bar lines are straight lines that divide the staff into measures or bars.

A **measure** or **bar** is a small section of the staff.

Time signatures are two numbers placed **beside the treble clef.** They tell us how many beats are allowed in each bar and show us how to count our music.

The **top number** tells us how many beats are allowed in each bar. The **bottom number** tells us what kind of note is counted as one beat. The 4 means quarter note, so in 4/4 time, we are allowed four beats in each bar and each beat is equal to a quarter note.

1. ✓ Look at the counting in these examples.

2. ✋ Clap and count the rhythms.

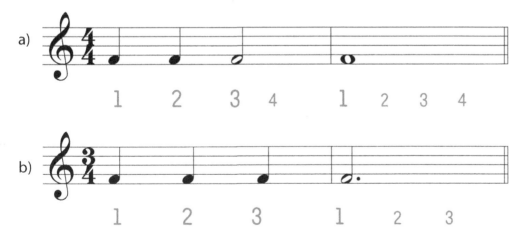

LESSON REVIEW: BAR LINES, MEASURES AND TIME SIGNATURES

1. ✏ Write your own rhythm on the staff below. *(6 marks)*

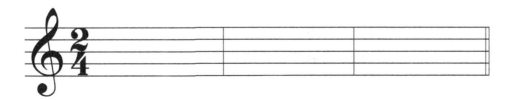

_____
6

Lesson Nine

EXERCISES MOVING IN STEPS

Date: _____

steps

| DO | RE | MI |

| C | D | E |

1.  Sing the following stepping exercises.

a)

i) What is this? _____

ii) What does it tell you to do? _____

b)

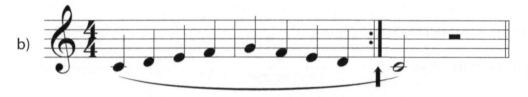

Discuss this symbol with your teacher.

ii) What is it called? _____

iii) What does it tell you to do? _____

INTERVALS

interval

An interval is the distance between two notes.
Singing and identifying intervals is important for all musicians.

The distance between **DO** and **RE** is called a **Major 2nd**.

DO RE

A **Major 2nd** sounds like:

the beginning of a scale.

_____

Music is also written using symbols called **rests**. A rest is a moment of silence. Just like notes, rests are counted using steady "**counts**" or "**beats**".

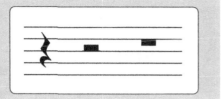

quarter rests

There is silence for **one** beat or count.

1. Practice drawing **quarter rests** on the staff.

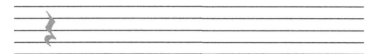

half rest

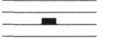

There is silence for **two** beats or counts.

2. What space is the **half rest** in? _____

3. Practice drawing **half rests** on the staff.

LESSON REVIEW: QUARTER RESTS AND HALF RESTS

1. Write the counts under the notes and rests. *(10 marks)*
2. Clap and count the rhythms. *(5 marks)*

a)

b)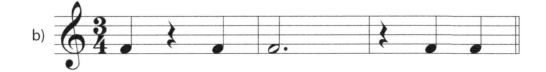

15

SINGING SKIPS AND TRIADS

Date: _____

| skips | | DO MI SO | C E G |

1. 🗣 Sing the following exercise.

a)

triad

A triad is a chord made up of the **first**, **third,** and **fifth** notes of a scale. The notes move from **line to line to line** or **space to space to space**. Sing triads slowly. Be careful not to "scoop" or "slide" into these skipping notes.

2. 🗣 Sing a **triad** the following ways.

☐ Using tonic sol-fa.

☐ Using a very slow tempo.

☐ Backwards (starting on the highest note).

INTERVALS

If you can sing a triad easily, then you can sing this interval.

The distance between **DO** and **MI** is called a **Major 3rd**.

A **Major 3rd** sounds like:

a triad.

_____

☐ I can identify 2nds and 3rds played or sung by my teacher.

There is silence
for **four** beats.

A **whole rest** also
indicates one entire
measure of silence in
any time signature.

1. What space is the **whole rest** in? _____

2. Practice drawing **whole rests** on the staff.

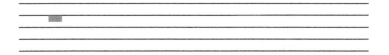

3. Write the counts underneath the notes and rests.

4. Clap and count the rhythms.

a)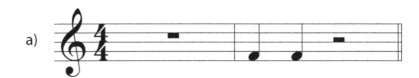

b)

c)

LESSON REVIEW: STEPS & SKIPS

1. Identify each pair of notes as a step or skip. *(7 marks)*

skip _____ _____ _____

_____ _____ _____

7

TECHNICAL EXERCISES

Date: _____

1.  Sing the following exercise confidently without assistance from the piano. *(4 marks)*

i) What does this symbol mean? _____

a)

_____
4

TONIC SOL-FA

| DO' |
| TI |
| LA |
| SO |
| FA |
| MI |
| RE |
| DO |

1. ✓ Check when completed.

☐ I can sing the tonic sol-fa scale **ascending** and **descending**. *(1 mark)*

☐ I can sing a triad **ascending** and **descending**. *(1 mark)*

☐ I can sing the following patterns. *(2 marks each)*

a)

DO RE   DO RE

b)

DO RE   MI FA SO

_____
6

INTERVALS

1. 🖊 Write the tonic sol-fa syllables that make a Major 2nd. _____ _____ *(1 mark)*

2. 🖊 Write the tonic sol-fa syllables that make a Major 3rd. _____ _____ *(1 mark)*

3. ☐ I can identify Major 2nds and Major 3rds played or sung by my teacher. *(3 marks)*

_____
5

. ✎ Write the counts underneath the rhythms. *(3 marks each)*

. ✋ Clap and count the following. *(2 marks each)*

i) What is this called? _____

a)

b)

$\overline{10}$

NOTE NAMES

. ✎ Write the sentence that helps you remember the line notes. *(1 mark)*

_____

. ✎ Write the word that helps you remember the space notes. *(1 mark)*

_____

. ✎ Name the notes. They spell words. *(5 marks)*

a)

A ___ ___ ___ ___ ___

$\overline{15}$ $\overline{40}$

Are you ready to perform a memorized song for your teacher?
Use a performance assessment form at the back of your book (page 54) to record your progress.

SIGHT SINGING

Date: _____

| sight singing | **Sight singing** means singing music for the first time without any assistance from the piano or another singer. Sight singing is a very important skill for every vocalist. |

✓ Before you begin:

☐ Always look over the music.

☐ Look at the time signature.

☐ Look and listen to your first note.

☐ Keep a slow and steady pace.

☐ Sing out confidently.

1. 🎤 Sing the **C major scale** *slowly* using the tonic sol-fa syllables.

D R M F S L T D' T L S F M R D

2. ✏️ Write the tonic sol-fa syllables under the notes. *(Optional)*

3. ✋ Clap and count the rhythms.

4. 🎤 Sight sing the following *slowly*.

i) What is the starting note? _____

a)

ii) What is the ending note? ____

b)

i) How many beats is this note? _____

. Identify intervals played or sung by your teacher.

. Sing the intervals after your teacher has given a starting note.

Interval	identify:	sing:
Major 2nd	☐	☐
Major 3rd	☐	☐

LESSON REVIEW: C MAJOR SCALE SOL-FA

1. ✎ Write the tonic sol-fa syllable for each note. *(5 marks)*

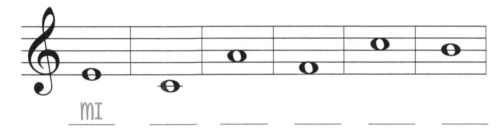

MI

2. ✎ Write the note on the staff that matches the tonic sol-fa syllable. *(5 marks)*

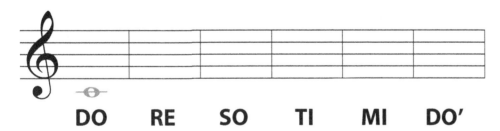

DO   RE   SO   TI   MI   DO'

3. ✎ Write your own sight singing exercise and have your teacher sing it back to you. *(5 marks)*

15

Lesson Twelve

SINGING STACCATO

Date: _____

staccato

Sing staccato! Staccato means short and detached. Staccato notes are marked with a dot above or below. Pay close attention to **articulation markings** that specify how individual notes are to be performed.

1. Describe the differences between staccato dots and a dotted half note.

_____

_____

2. Sing the following exercise slowly.

a)

SIGHT SINGING

1. Write the tonic sol-fa syllables under the notes. *(Optional)*
2. Clap and count the rhythms.
3. Sight sing the melodies.

i) How many beats are in each bar? _____

a)

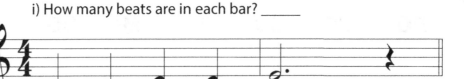

i) What is the highest note? _____

b)

30   FULL VOICE WORKBOOK - LEVEL ONE

. 🖉 Identify songs or short melodies that will help you to remember this interval.

The distance between **DO** and **FA** is called a **Perfect 4th**.

A **Perfect 4th** sounds like:

_____

_____

. 👂 Identify intervals played or sung by your teacher.

. 🗣 Sing the intervals after your teacher has given a starting note.

Interval	tonic sol-fa:	identify:	sing:
Major 2nd	____ to ____	☐	☐
Major 3rd	____ to ____	☐	☐
Perfect 4th	____ to ____	☐	☐

LESSON REVIEW: WRITING NOTES WITH DOTS

1. 🖉 Write each note on the staff using **dotted half notes**. *(2 marks each)*

F   **G**   **D**   **C**   **A**

2. 🖉 Add **staccato dots** to each note. *(2 marks)*

10

SINGING WITH DYNAMICS

Date: _____

dynamics	Dynamics refer to the **volume** that the music is being sung. Different volumes are marked in your music by different music symbols. **Singing with dynamics makes a performance exciting.**

This is a **crescendo** marking.
It means to gradually sing louder.

This is a **decrescendo** marking.
It means to gradually sing softer.

1. Sing the following exercises using dynamics:

a)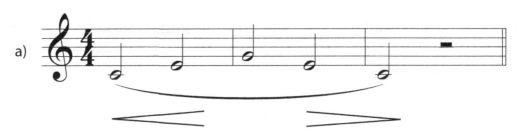

b)

SIGHT SINGING

1. Answer the questions below. 2. Clap and count the rhythms.

3. Sight sing the following.

i) What is this? _____   ii) What is this? _____

a)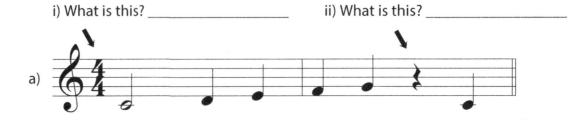

i) What is the starting note? _____

b)

Find the group of **two black keys** on the piano keyboard.

C is to the *left* of the two black keys.

D is the middle white key.

E is to the *right* of the two black keys.

1. Circle the groups of two black keys on this keyboard.

2. Label **C**, **D,** and **E** on this keyboard.

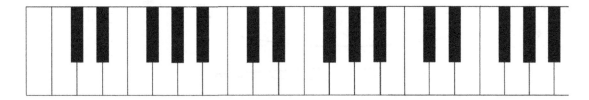

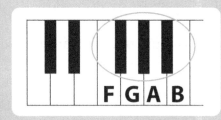

Find the group of **three black keys** on the piano keyboard.

F is to the *left* of the three black keys.

G is between the first and second black key.

A is between the second and third black key.

B is to the *right* of the three black keys.

3. Circle the groups of three black keys on this keyboard.

4. Label **F**, **G**, **A,** and **B** on this keyboard.

LESSON REVIEW: THE PIANO KEYBOARD

1. Name each dotted piano key. *(7 marks)*

$\overline{}$
7

Lesson Fourteen

TECHNICAL EXERCISES

Date: _____

1. 💬 Explain the music markings to your teacher.

2. 🗣 Sing the following exercises.

a)

b)
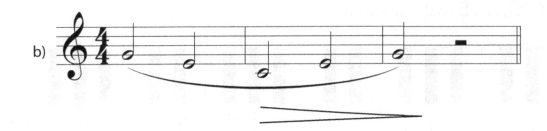

INTERVALS

If you can sing ascending and descending triads easily, then you can use this familiar exercise to sing these intervals.

Ascending:

 The distance between **DO** and **MI** is a **Major 3rd**.

A **Major 3rd** sounds like:

a triad.

_____

 The distance between **DO** and **SO** is called a **Perfect 5th**.

A **Perfect 5th** sounds like:

_____

_____

Descending:

 The distance between **SO** and **MI** is called a **minor 3rd**.

A **minor 3rd** sounds like:

_____

_____

1. Name each dotted piano key.

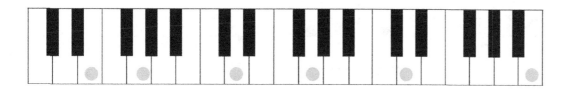

BEAMED EIGHTH NOTES

beamed eighth notes

♪♪

½   ½

An eighth note is held for **half a beat** or count. Two eighth notes equal one beat.

Two or more eighth notes are connected with a **beam**.

Eighth notes are counted **"one-and two-and"**.

When there are more than two eighth notes beamed together, the counting is the same.

1. Practice drawing **beamed eighth notes**.

2. ✓ Check when completed.

☐ I can clap and count eighth notes with my teacher.

☐ I can clap and count eighth notes by myself.

☐ I can clap and count alternating between eighth notes and quarter notes.

Lesson Fifteen

1.  Sing the following exercises.

a)

b)

c)

INTERVAL REVIEW

1. Identify intervals played or sung by your teacher.

2. Sing the intervals after your teacher has given a starting note.

Ascending	identify:	sing:	**Descending**	identify:	sing:
Major 2nd	☐	☐	minor 3rd	☐	☐
Major 3rd	☐	☐			
Perfect 4th	☐	☐			
Perfect 5th	☐	☐			

. 🖉 How long is an eighth note held for? _____

. 🖉 Write the counts underneath the rhythm.

. ✋ Clap and count the notes with your teacher.

. ✋ Clap and count the notes by yourself.

a)

. 🖉 Write the counts underneath the rhythms.

. ✋ Clap and count the notes slowly.

a)

b)

LESSON REVIEW: BEAMED EIGHTH NOTES

1. 🖉 Write the counts underneath the rhythms. *(5 marks)*

2. ✋ Clap and count the rhythms slowly. *(5 marks)*

a)

b)

10

Review Three

TECHNICAL EXERCISES

Date: _____

1. Sing the following exercises slowly. *(3 marks each)*

i) This exercise is called a: **scale**   **triad**   (circle one)

a)

b)

— 6

CLAPPING AND COUNTING

1. Write the counts underneath the rhythms. *(3 marks)*

2. Clap and count the notes slowly. *(3 marks)*

a)

— 6

SIGHT SINGING

1. Sight sing the following. *(5 marks)*

a)

— 5

. 🎧 Identify intervals played or sung by your teacher. *(4 marks)*

. 🗣 Sing the intervals after your teacher has given a starting note. *(4 marks)*

Ascending	identify:	sing:	**Descending**	identify:	sing:
Major 2nd	☐	☐	minor 3rd	☐	☐
Major 3rd	☐	☐			
Perfect 4th	☐	☐			
Perfect 5th	☐	☐			

___
8

MUSIC THEORY

. ✏ Write each note on the staff using **dotted half notes**. *(4 marks)*

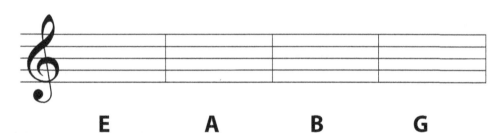

E   A   B   G

. ✏ Write the correct letter names on each piano key. *(6 marks)*

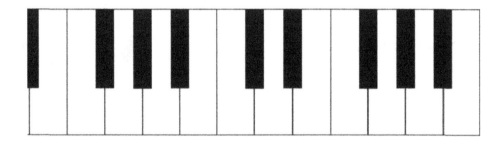

___
10  35

Are you ready to perform a memorized song for your teacher?
Use a performance assessment form at the back of your book (page 54) to record your progress.

Lesson Sixteen

arpeggio	An arpeggio is a chord made up of the **first**, **third**, **fifth** and **eighth** notes of a scale. Sing arpeggios slowly. Be careful not to "scoop" or "slide" into these skipping notes.

1. 🎤 Sing the arpeggio *slowly*.

a)

2. ✏️ Does this exercise move in steps or skips? _____

3. 💬 What is the difference between a triad and an arpeggio?

4. ✓ Check when completed.

   ☐ I can sing a descending arpeggio.

   ☐ I can sing a descending triad.

SEMITONES

semitone	A **semitone (or half step)** is the smallest interval. It is the distance from one key on the piano to the very next key with no key in between.

1. ✏️ Mark semitones on the piano keyboard.

   a) From a white key to a black key.

   b) From a black key to a white key.

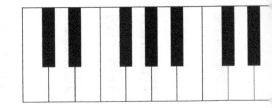

2. ✏️ Mark semitones on the piano keyboard.

   a) From a white key to a white key (there are two).

   b) Name the notes.

_____ _____ and _____ _____

An **accidental** is a symbol placed before a note to change its pitch by a semitone.

sharp

Raises a note by a semitone.

1. Draw **sharps** beside the following notes.

2. Name the notes below the staff.

3. Play the notes on the piano keyboard.

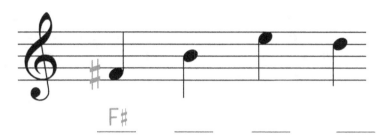

F#

flat

Lowers a note by a semitone.

4. Draw **flats** beside the following notes.

5. Name the notes below the staff.

6. Play the notes on the piano keyboard.

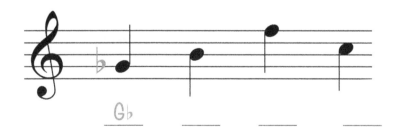

Gb

natural

Cancels a sharp or a flat.

7. Draw **naturals** beside the following notes.

8. Name the notes below the staff.

9. Play the notes on the piano keyboard.

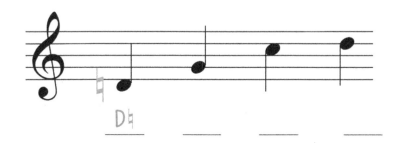

D♮

TECHNICAL EXERCISES

Date: _____

Lesson Seventeen

1. Sing the following exercises.

   i) This exercise is called a: **scale   triad   arpeggio** (circle one).

   a)

   i) This exercise is called: **an arpeggio   a scale   a triad** (circle one).

   b)

2. ✓ Check when completed.

   ☐ I can sing a descending arpeggio.

   ☐ I can sing a descending triad.

CLAPPING AND COUNTING

1. Clap and count the following exercise.

   a)

SIGHT SINGING

1. Sight sing the following exercise.

   a)

Name the notes on the keyboard.

a) using **sharps**.

b) using **flats**.

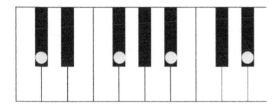

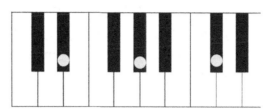

Name the notes on the staff.

LESSON REVIEW: ACCIDENTALS

1. Write the notes on the staff. Use **half notes**. (5 marks)

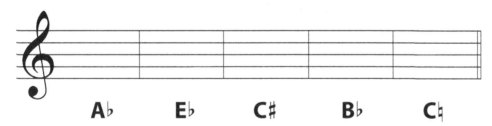

2. Mark an X on the following notes on the piano keyboard. (7 marks)

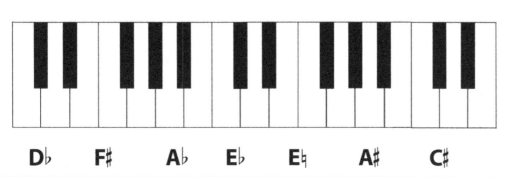

12

SINGING WITH DYNAMICS: pp - ff   Date: _____

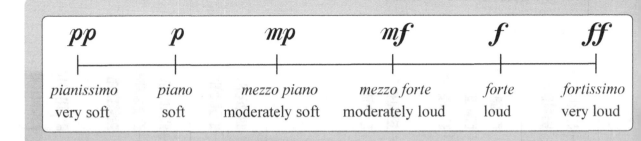

pp	p	mp	mf	f	ff
pianissimo	*piano*	*mezzo piano*	*mezzo forte*	*forte*	*fortissimo*
very soft	soft	moderately soft	moderately loud	loud	very loud

1. ✓ Study the different dynamic symbols above.

2. 🗣 Sing this exercise using different dynamics.

a)

3. ✓ Look at a piece from your repertoire.

   a) ✎ Circle all dynamic markings with a pencil.

   b) ✎ Add some of your own dynamic markings to this piece.

   c) 🗣 Perform this piece for your teacher focusing on performing all
      the dynamic markings.

   d) 💬 Discuss with your teacher why the composer decided to use these dynamics.

INTERVALS REVIEW

1. 👂 Identify intervals played or sung by your teacher.

2. 🗣 Sing the intervals after your teacher has given a starting note.

Ascending	identify:	sing:	**Descending**	identify:	sing:
Major 2nd	☐	☐	minor 3rd	☐	☐
Major 3rd	☐	☐			
Perfect 4th	☐	☐			
Perfect 5th	☐	☐			

NOTES ON THE MUSIC STAFF AND PIANO KEYBOARD

Middle C is a special note on the staff and piano keyboard.

1. ✓ With your teacher, look at middle C on the staff and on the piano keyboard.
2. 🗣 Name the notes on the staff.
3. ✏ Draw a line to the correct note on the piano keyboard.

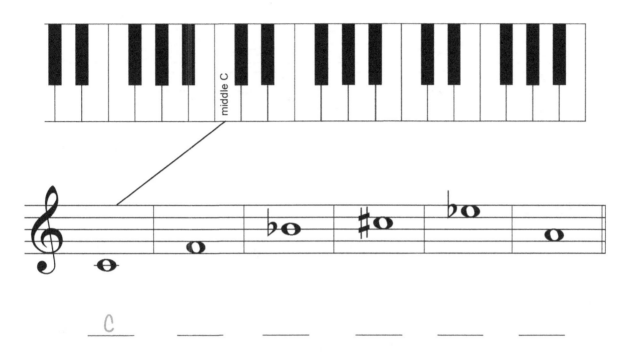

middle C

C ___ ___ ___ ___ ___ ___

LESSON REVIEW: NOTES ON THE STAFF AND PIANO KEYBOARD

1. ✏ Name the notes with a dot on the piano keyboard. *(3 marks)*

2. ✏ Write the notes on the staff below. *(4 marks)*

a)
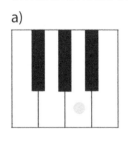

b)
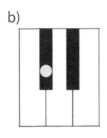

c)
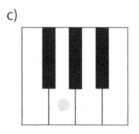

d)
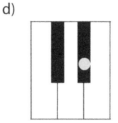

A ___   ___   ___

7

TECHNICAL EXERCISES

Date: _____

1. 🎤 Sing the following exercises.

a)

b)

INTERVALS

If you can sing ascending and descending arpeggios easily, then you can use this familiar exercis
to sing these intervals.

Ascending:

The distance between **DO** and **High DO'** is called a **Perfect octave**.

DO DO'

An ascending **Perfect octave** sounds like:

_____

_____

Descending:

The distance between **High DO'** and **DO** is a **descending Perfect octave**.

DO' DO

A descending **Perfect octave** sounds like:

_____

_____

The distance between **High DO** and **SO** is a **descending Perfect 4th**.

DO' SO

A descending **Perfect 4th** sounds like:

_____

_____

RHYTHM READING

. ✓ Look carefully at the rhythm examples below.

. 👂 Listen carefully as your teacher performs the following one-bar rhythm
     examples **at random**. Can you identify the correct rhythm?

a)

b)

c)

d)

SIGHT SINGING

. 🗣 Sight sing the following melodies.

a)

b)

Are you ready to perform a mini-recital for your teacher and family?
Use the mini-recital assessment form at the back of your book (page 55) to record your progress.

TECHNICAL EXERCISES

Date: _____

fermata

Hold the note longer than its written value.

1. Sing the following exercises.

a)

breath mark

,

It tells the singer where to breathe in a phrase.

b)

2. ✓ Check when completed.

☐ I can find a fermata in my repertoire.

☐ I can find a breath mark in my repertoire.

SIGHT SINGING

1. Clap and count the rhythms.
2. Sight sing the melodies.

i) What is the starting note? _____   ii) What is the ending note? _____

a)

i) Write a fermata above the highest note.

b)

1. Identify intervals played or sung by your teacher.

2. Sing the intervals after your teacher has given a starting note.

Ascending	tonic sol-fa:	identify:	sing:
Major 2nd	____ to ____	☐	☐
Major 3rd	____ to ____	☐	☐
Perfect 4th	____ to ____	☐	☐
Perfect 5th	____ to ____	☐	☐
Perfect octave	____ to ____	☐	☐
Descending			
minor 3rd	____ to ____	☐	☐
Perfect 4th	____ to ____	☐	☐
Perfect octave	____ to ____	☐	☐

1. Name the notes on the staff.

2. Draw a line from the note on the staff to its piano key.

3. Play the notes on the piano.

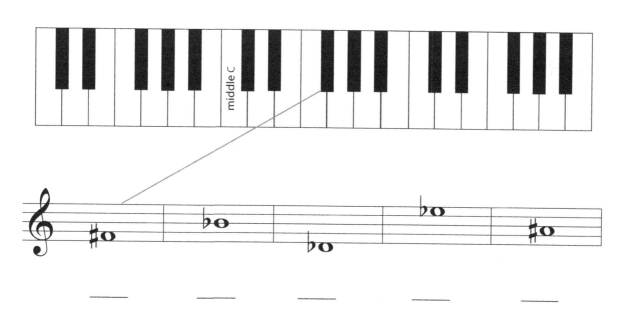

TECHNICAL EXERCISES

Date: _____

1. Sing the following exercise without assistance from the piano. *(1 mark)*

a)

2. ✓ Check when completed.

☐ I can sing a triad with tonic sol-fa syllables. *(1 mark)*

☐ I can sing a triad without tonic sol-fa syllables. *(1 mark)*

☐ I can sing an arpeggio. *(1 mark)*

4

INTERVALS

1. Sing the intervals after your teacher has given a starting note. *(1 mark each)*

Ascending	sing:	**Descending**	sing:
Major 2nd	☐	minor 3rd	☐
Major 3rd	☐	Perfect 4th	☐
Perfect 4th	☐	Perfect octave	☐
Perfect 5th	☐		
Perfect octave	☐		

8

SIGHT SINGING

1. Identify the tonic sol-fa syllables aloud. *(5 marks)*

2. Clap and count the rhythms. *(Optional)*

3. Sight sing the following. *(5 marks)*

a)

10

. 🖉 Draw the rests on the staff. *(3 marks)*

       a) half rest   b) quarter rest   c) whole rest

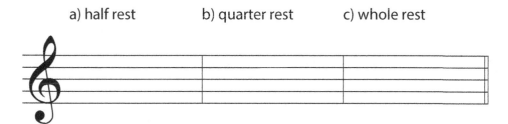

. 🖉 Name the notes. *(5 marks)*

_____   _____   _____   _____   _____

. 🖉 Write the notes on the staff below. *(5 marks)*

. 🖉 Draw lines connecting each note on the staff to the correct piano key. *(5 marks)*

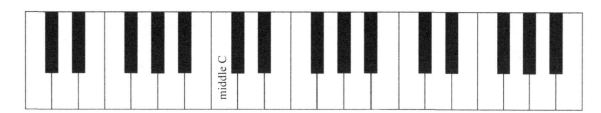

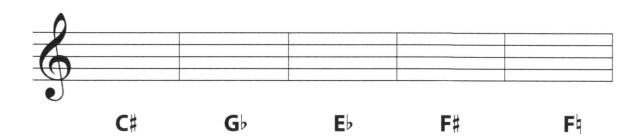

      C♯   **G♭**   **E♭**   **F♯**   **F♮**

$$\frac{18}{} \quad \frac{40}{}$$

ADDITIONAL RHYTHM READING EXERCISES

1.  Clap and count the rhythms.

2.  Clap and count the rhythms.

Sight sing the following.

a) **DO** **DO** **RE** **DO** **RE** **MI**

b) **DO** **RE** **MI** **MI** **FA** **SO**

c) **MI** **RE** **DO** **DO** **RE** **MI**

d) **DO** **RE** **RE** **MI** **FA** **FA**

e) **MI** **FA** **SO** **SO** **FA** **MI**

Sight sing the following.

a)

b)

c)

d)

Performance Assessments

PERFORMANCE ASSESSMENT #2   Date: _____

Choose one memorized song and perform it for your teacher.

Performances will be marked accordingly: **A Great job** – keep up the good work.

                                           B Good job – still room to improve.

                                           C Needs work – improvement needed here.

Song: _____

1. Did the singer appear comfortable and confident?   **A   B   C**

2. Did the singer sing/speak clearly throughout the song?   **A   B   C**

3. Did the performer sing smoothly?   **A   B   C**

4. Did the singer avoid scoops and slides?   **A   B   C**

5. Did the singer perform all notes and rhythms accurately? **A   B   C**

Teacher comments:

PERFORMANCE ASSESSMENT # 3   Date: _____

Choose one memorized song and perform it for your teacher.

Performances will be marked accordingly: **A Great job** – keep up the good work.

                                           B Good job – still room to improve.

                                           C Needs work – improvement needed here.

Song: _____

1. Did the singer introduce the song?   **A   B   C**

2. Did the singer sing/speak clearly throughout the song?   **A   B   C**

3. Did the singer use contrasting dynamics?   **A   B   C**

4. Was this performance expressive and exciting?   **A   B   C**

Teacher comments:

Date: _____

Choose two or more songs and perform for your teacher, friends and family.

Record this performance so that teacher and student can review/discuss together.

Performances will be marked accordingly: **A** **Great job** – keep up the good work.

                                                                       B **Good job** – still room to improve.

                                                                       C **Needs work** – improvement needed here.

Songs: _____ Composer: _____

        _____ Composer: _____

        _____ Composer: _____

1. Did the singer appear comfortable and confident?   **A**   **B**   **C**

2. Did the singer use an introduction for the songs?   **A**   **B**   **C**

3. Was this performance expressive and exciting?   **A**   **B**   **C**

4. Did this performer use contrasting dynamics effectively?   **A**   **B**   **C**

5. Did the singer use good vocal technique?   **A**   **B**   **C**

6. How has this performer improved?

_____

_____

_____

7. What can this performer do to continuing improving?

_____

_____

8. Students, how did you feel about your performance?

_____

_____

_____

REPERTOIRE LIST

Use this form to record all songs that you have learned and can perform from memory.

Date	Song	Composer	Performance
Sept 23	Lullaby	Nancy Telfer	Recital piece

1. Suggested listening/learning (new vocalists or repertoire to discover).

   _____

   _____

   _____

2. Teacher comments.

   _____

   _____

Made in the USA
Las Vegas, NV
29 January 2024

85087470R00033